Contents

Heat from underground

The origins of geothermal energy are deep inside the Earth. The word geothermal comes from the Greek words *ge* (meaning Earth) and *therme* (heat), and the energy is produced by the planet's natural heat. There is geothermal energy all over the world, and in many regions it can be used in large quantities. Experts believe it could be a very important energy source for the future.

Beneath the crust

The inside of our planet is made up of four sections. If we could travel to the centre of the Earth, we would notice the temperature rising throughout our journey. We live on Earth's hard outer layer, called the crust, which acts as the planet's skin. The crust is not equally thick all the way around, but varies from a depth of about 40 kilometres under the land of the continents to eight kilometres under the oceans.

The crust is made of different kinds of rocks, and if we could bore our way down, we would find that the temperature increases by about 30°C per kilometre for the first ten kilometres. This shows how much heat is stored beneath the surface. Rock is a very poor conductor of heat, so the crust acts as a form of insulation, keeping much of the heat inside the planet.

From mantle to core

Beneath the Earth's crust is a 2900-kilometre thick layer of mainly molten rock, called the mantle. This makes up more than three quarters of the planet's volume. The temperature of the mantle rises to between 700 and 900°C in the upper part, and to more than 4000°C at the bottom.

ENERGY

Neil Morris

W
FRANKLIN WATTS
LONDON•SYDNEY

An Appleseed Editions book

First published in 2009 by Franklin Watts
338 Euston Road, London NW1 3BH

Franklin Watts Australia
Hachette Children's Books
Level 17/207 Kent St, Sydney, NSW 2000

© 2009 Appleseed Editions

Created by Appleseed Editions Ltd,
Well House, Friars Hill, Guestling,
East Sussex TN35 4ET

Designed by Helen James
Edited by Mary-Jane Wilkins
Artwork by Guy Callaby
Picture research by Su Alexander

ISBN 978 07496 8772 4

Dewey Classification: 333.8'8

A CIP catalogue for this book is available from the British Library.

Photograph acknowledgements
page 8 Corbis; 11 Arctic- Images/Corbis; 12 Kennan Ward/Corbis; 13 Roger
Ressmeyer/Corbis; 15 Steven Vidler/Eurasia Press/Corbis; 17 Catherine Karnow/
Corbis; 18 Kevin R Morris/Corbis; 19 Atlantide Phototravel/Corbis; 21 Paul Souders/
Corbis; 22 Roger Ressmeyer/Corbis; 23 Arctic-Images/Corbis; 24 Annette
Soumillard/Hemis/Corbis; 30 Roger Ressmeyer/Corbis; 31 Bob Rowan; Progressive
Image/Corbis; 33 Geopower Basel AG;Fischer & Ryser; 35 Raymond Gehman/
Corbis; 37 Michael S Yamashita/Corbis; 38 Gary Braasch/Corbis; 39 Mark Newham;
Eye Ubiquitous/Corbis; 41 Barbara Walton/epa/Corbis; 42 Chenahotsprings.com
Front cover Annette Soumillard/Hemis/Corbis
Printed in China

Franklin Watts is a division of Hachette Children's Books,
an Hachette Livre UK company.
www.hachettelivre.co.uk

This cutaway illustration shows the four different sections that make up the Earth's interior. The numbers give the diameter of the inner core and the width of the other three layers. The total distance from the Earth's surface to its centre is nearly 6500 km.

The molten rock moves very slowly, carrying heat towards the Earth's surface, cooling and then sinking to heat up again. The rock sinks towards the Earth's core, which is made up of two layers. The outer core is more than 2000 kilometres thick and consists of molten iron and nickel. Its temperature can be 6000°C. Beneath this layer the pressure is so great that the metal – which is mainly iron – is solid. This iron sphere is about 2600 kilometres across – just a little bigger than the Moon. The temperature of the inner core may be as high as 7000°C, which is hotter than the surface of the Sun.

Inner core
1300 km

Outer core
2250 km

Mantle
2900 km

Crust
8 to 40 km

Why is the Earth hot inside?

There are several reasons for this. Heat was left over when the planet was formed about 4.6 billion years ago. After the Sun formed, gas and dust spinning around it collided and stuck together, making planets, including the Earth. The creation of the Earth caused friction and this made it a hot molten ball which is still cooling. The denser, heavier parts sank towards the centre of the planet, creating more friction and more heat. Since then, radioactive elements (such as uranium) in the Earth's mantle and crust have been releasing energy particles in a process called radioactive decay. This process gives off huge amounts of energy in the form of heat, and this makes up most of today's geothermal energy.

GEOTHERMAL POWER

A fountain of lava spurts out of Kilauea volcano, on the island of Hawaii. This huge volcano appears above a hot spot in the Earth's crust (see page 11).

Letting out the heat

The Earth's solid, rocky crust keeps the planet's heat in. But it is not completely sealed, because the crust is not made of one continuous layer of rocks. It is cracked into huge pieces, called tectonic plates (from the Greek *tekton*, meaning builder). The plates fit together like a giant jigsaw. Heat rises into the crust through the upper part of the mantle, called the asthenosphere, on which the plates sit. The magma (or molten mantle rock) cools and slowly sinks again over millions of years. At the same time, the moving magma shifts the tectonic plates. Plates move very slowly – a few centimetres a year.

Piping hot

An American geology professor has calculated that on average enough heat comes up through the Earth's crust to make three cups of hot coffee every minute for all the world's 6.7 billion inhabitants. That's 1.2 trillion cups of coffee every hour!

Volcanic world

As the Earth's plates move, they rub against each other. This squeezing and buckling of plates can create volcanoes. They are openings in the Earth's crust where magma forces its way through cracks to the surface. The streams of molten rock that reach the surface are called lava. Many volcanoes are caused by an oceanic plate being forced under a neighbouring continental plate. This happens at a place called a convergent or destructive margin in a region known as a subduction zone. Forces cause cracks in the

Will the Earth's heat ever run out?

Yes, it will, but not for a very long time. The Earth and especially the mantle have been losing heat for some time, but in tiny amounts. At the same time, the planet's solid inner core has been expanding very slowly (some scientists say by about one centimetre every thousand years). And geologists believe that the core's expansion is releasing more heat into the mantle.

Nevertheless, the overall cooling will continue by tiny amounts for billions of years. The cooling will harden the asthenosphere and tectonic plates may stop moving. But before it cools completely, in approximately another 5 billion years, the Earth will have stopped receiving energy from the Sun, which will cool and swell up into a red giant star.

continental crust that become volcanoes. As the descending plate slips down into the asthenosphere, its rocks melt back into the mantle and are recycled. The huge forces often produce massive earthquakes.

The ultimate energy source

All our energy comes from the Sun, which makes it the ultimate energy source. This is also true for geothermal energy, because the Earth would not have formed (and would not have been hot) if its original material had not been sent spinning around a new star – the Sun. Without the Sun there would also be no weather on Earth and therefore no water cycle. And without water, we would not be able to use geothermal energy in the way we do – for heating or generating electricity.

A map of the world's major tectonic plates. The arrows show the direction in which the plates generally move. At a transform margin, the plates slide past one another.

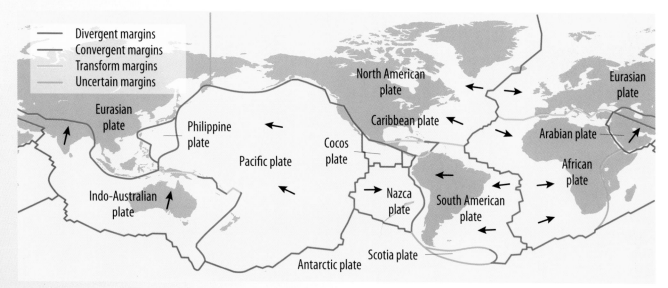

Divergent margins
Convergent margins
Transform margins
Uncertain margins

Eurasian plate
Philippine plate
Pacific plate
Indo-Australian plate
North American plate
Caribbean plate
Cocos plate
Nazca plate
South American plate
Scotia plate
Antarctic plate
Eurasian plate
Arabian plate
African plate

The Ring of Fire runs right around the Pacific Ocean. Because of the enormous forces involved, the whole region experiences earthquakes as well as volcanoes.

Eurasian plate

North American plate

Gorda plate

Philippine plate

Caroline plate

Pacific plate

Cocos plate

Fiji plate

PACIFIC OCEAN

Indo-Australian plate

Nazca plate

South American plate

Ring of Fire

Antarctic plate

Ring of Fire

The main volcanic regions of the world are all near the edge of plates. These regions can produce the most geothermal power, as the Earth's heat comes right up to the surface at these points. Many of them lie in a huge belt around the edges of the Pacific Ocean, known as the Ring of Fire. This runs around the boundaries of the huge Pacific plate. To the west, the Ring of Fire runs from Japan down through the islands of southeast Asia to New Zealand. On the other side of the ocean, the Ring goes from Alaska down the length of the North American coast to the Andes mountains of South America. There are subduction zones on both sides of the ocean.

Making new crust

As well as crashing together, plates can move apart. They do this beneath the oceans, leaving a crack where magma comes to the surface, cools, hardens and creates new crust. This process creates more than two square kilometres of new ocean crust every year in regions called divergent or constructive margins. The areas of new hardened magma are known as spreading ridges.

Sometimes the peaks of a ridge appear above the ocean surface and form islands. The best examples lie on the Mid-Atlantic Ridge, which stretches for about 16,000 kilometres, from north-east of Greenland to level with the southern tip of South America. Islands on the North Atlantic stretch of the ridge include Iceland and the Azores, both of which have large amounts of geothermal energy. In Iceland, the two plates are moving apart at about two centimetres per year.

Plumes and hot spots

Plates often move by about ten centimetres every year. You can see this in parts of the world where hot, molten rocks come near to the surface and are called mantle plumes. They form areas called hot spots. As a plate moves over the spot (which is stationary) magma burns through the thin crust and creates a volcano. This movement causes a series of volcanoes. The Hawaiian islands were created in this way.

Drilling through the crust

Scientists have learned about geothermal heat from drilling projects. One day it might even be possible to drill right down to the mantle and tap into the intense heat there. Until now, the deepest hole ever drilled is the Kola Superdeep Borehole, on a peninsula in north-west Russia. Drilling began in 1970, and by 1983 had reached a depth of 12,000 metres. It was another six years before the drill reached its deepest point – 12,262 metres – the world record depth to this day. The temperature at that depth was 180°C, which was higher than the expected 100°C. Drilling stopped in 1992. The hole went about a third of the way down into the continental crust, drilling into hot rocks which are about 2.7 billion years old. Future projects might concentrate on oceanic crust, which is generally much thinner.

This photograph of the Mid-Atlantic Ridge in Thingvellir National Park in Iceland shows clearly where two plates are slowly moving apart.

GEOTHERMAL POWER

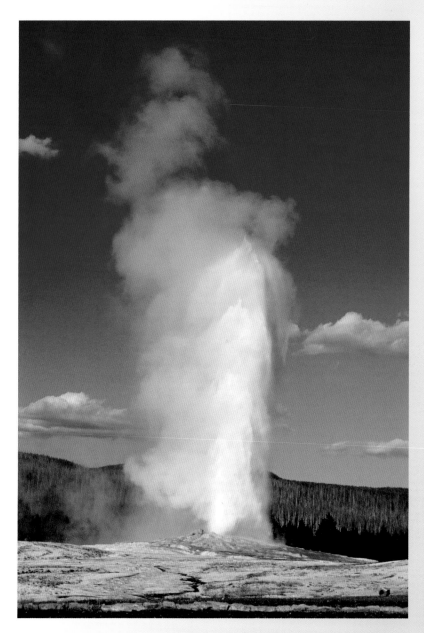

Old Faithful geyser, in Yellowstone National Park, USA, erupts every 60-90 minutes. This region's geysers are very popular with tourists, who have to stay a safe distance away from the hot water and steam.

Hot springs and geysers

The water in hot springs (also called thermal springs) is heated by hot molten rock that lies near the surface. Cold rainwater trickles down through cracks until it reaches rocks that have been heated up by magma. The hot, steaming water rises back up to the surface, where it may form a warm pool or stream. Some springs build up a great force in deep channels, where the hot water cannot easily boil and turn to steam because of the weight of cooler water above it (increased pressure raises the boiling point of a liquid). The channels usually go down at least 2000 metres.

When it does eventually boil, the steam rises quickly and forces hot water, steam and air ahead of it. Jets of steam and boiling water explode out of a crack or hole. The most explosive ones shoot water more than 100 metres into the air. The jet of water usually lasts for a few seconds before the crack fills up and the process starts all over again.

Icelandic gusher

Geysers are named after the Great Geysir in Iceland, which was probably first reported in the fourteenth century. In Icelandic, *geysir* means 'gusher'. The original geyser erupted every hour until the early twentieth century, when it stopped. Earthquakes in 2000 reactivated the geyser and it now gushes every eight to ten hours, reaching a height of 61 metres.

Power versus beauty

Many of the volcanic regions of the world with hot springs and geysers form beautiful landscapes. Some are national parks and have become important tourist attractions. The most famous is Yellowstone National Park, in north-west USA. The US National Park Service says that the 9000-sq km park has more geothermal features than any other place on Earth: 'With half of the Earth's geothermal features, Yellowstone holds the planet's most diverse and intact collection of geysers, hot springs, mud pots, and fumaroles. Its more than 300 geysers make up two thirds of all those found on Earth. Combine this with more than 10,000 thermal features, comprised of brilliantly colored hot springs, bubbling mud pots, and steaming fumaroles, and you have a place like no other.'

Yellowstone became the first US national park in 1872, when 300 people visited, and just over a hundred years later it was made a World Heritage Site by the United Nations. Since 1990 almost three million tourists have visited the park every year. It would be difficult to use the geothermal energy of the region without spoiling the landscape and the pleasure of millions of people.

Fumaroles and mud pots

Fumaroles are holes in the ground that give off steam and gases such as carbon dioxide and hydrogen sulphide. When steam forces its way to the surface through layers of volcanic ash and clay, it may bubble and plop in a mud pot. There are large areas of fumaroles and mud pots in volcanic regions of Iceland, New Zealand and the United States – including Yellowstone National Park.

Fumaroles spout gases on the Italian island of Vulcano, near Sicily. The island was named after the Roman god of fire, Vulcan, who also gave his name to volcanoes.

From ancient baths to modern spas

Scientists did not truly understand plate tectonics and the way the Earth's interior worked until the early twentieth century. Yet long before then people were taking advantage of the Earth's heat, using geothermal steam and hot springs for bathing and heating.

Ancient Greek ideas

The Greek philosopher Empedocles (495-435 BC) believed that the world was made up of four elements – air, earth, fire and water. The element of fire brought about volcanoes. Plato (427-347 BC) had slightly different ideas. He said that rivers of hot and cold water flowed through subterranean channels, where there was also fire, mud and lava. Aristotle (384-322 BC) thought that air was sucked into caves, where it was heated by underground fires. Eventually the hot air was forced to the surface, causing volcanoes and earthquakes. The ancient Greek philosophers were on the right track, but knew nothing of tectonic activity.

Earth gods and goddesses

People of many different cultures worshipped the Earth and its life-giving forces. The ancient Egyptians honoured Geb as an Earth deity and father of the gods. In ancient Greece and Rome, the Earth deity was female. The Greek Gaia was the daughter of Chaos, and Roman Tellus was also known as Terra Mater, or Mother Earth.

Roman baths

The ancient Romans were the first to use hot springs to supply bathing houses. One of their famous baths was built in England. Historians believe that the Romans may have come across a warm spring that had earlier been a sacred place to Celtic Britons, where they worshipped Sulis, the Celtic goddess of healing. The Romans called their settlement Aquae Sulis

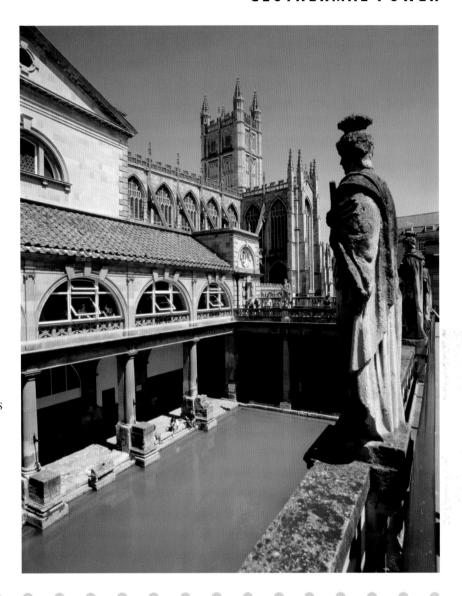

The Roman thermal bath house at Bath, in western England. It is overlooked by a later Christian abbey.

(waters of Sulis) and around AD 65 they built a temple there dedicated to their own goddess of medicine and wisdom, Minerva. They also constructed a lead-lined stone chamber around the sacred spring and a large rectangular bath, which was fed by the spring's warm waters. The Romans later included a caldarium (hot bath), tepidarium (warm bath), and frigidarium (cold bath). These are now part of the city of Bath, in Somerset.

Thermal bathing today

People still believe that thermal bathing is good for them. Some doctors think that the warmth and mineral properties of thermal water can help treat rheumatic disorders, skin ailments and respiratory problems. In Bath, you can still visit the Roman baths, although you can no longer bathe in them. In 2006, a complex of thermal baths opened in a new building. The operators say: 'Thermae Bath Spa is a day spa where you can bathe in the warm, natural mineral-rich waters and choose from a range of spa treatments designed to ease the body and soothe the mind. The water from these springs is believed to have fallen as rain around 10,000 years ago and then sank to a depth of about two kilometres below the Earth's surface. Here it was heated by high-temperature rocks before rising back up through a break in the limestone that lies beneath the city of Bath. More than one million litres of mineral-rich water flow from the thermal springs each day, at an average temperature of 45°C.'

Taking the cure

People who believed that thermal waters could help with medical problems began 'taking the cure' by visiting hot springs. The small village of Barèges, 1250 metres up in the Pyrenees mountains of south-western France, became a cure resort during the seventeenth century. This was two centuries after a farmer found an injured sheep bathing in a warm pool and noticed that the animal recovered well from its injuries. We now know that hot thermal waters rise to the surface at Barèges along a fault line between two different kinds of rock, granite and schist. The waters became more widely known in 1675 when members of the French royal family went to the village to bathe in hot baths and mud rich in sulphur and other minerals. During the nineteenth century, the thermal baths became part of a hospital which treated war wounds, rheumatism and skin problems.

Bathing for health

Medical treatment in thermal springs came to be known as balneotherapy (from the Latin balnium, meaning bath), or medicinal bathing. Although many people have reported pain relief from balneotherapy, scientific studies have not been able to prove that the therapy is as effective as some claim.

Spa resorts

Many European towns began to specialize in offering cures at their baths. Some, such as Aachen and Baden-Baden in Germany, became more famous than Barèges. Another was the small Belgian town of Spa, in the Ardennes hills near Liège. The town had been known for its hot springs since the fourteenth century, and became so famous that by 1600 the word spa was used to describe any resort with mineral springs. Bath, for example, became known as a spa, and the term is now in general use.

Native American springs

There are many hot springs in North and South America, and archaeologists have found evidence that Native Americans were using them many thousands of years ago. They must have used them for

Swimmers enjoy the thermal pool of the Gellert bath in Budapest, the capital of Hungary. The city has 188 thermal springs, and this bath opened in 1918.

warm bathing and may also have seen them as a source of healing. The different tribes probably saw springs as neutral regions, where they could live and bathe together in peace. One such place was Tonopah in Arizona, named by the early Hohokam people and meaning 'hot water under the bush'. The springs came from a large underground source.

Have hot springs always had a positive image?

Not really, because some people have associated them with natural disasters, such as volcanic eruptions and earthquakes. Historians believe that the Native Americans of the California region bathed in the local hot springs for their health and possibly as part of a ritual ceremony. But when the explorer William Bell Elliot stumbled upon a steaming valley of Californian fumaroles in 1847, he reported that he had discovered the 'gates of hell'. He called the region the Geysers (though what he'd found were fumaroles), and this was to eventually become the largest complex of geothermal power plants in the world (see page 30).

American resorts

During the 1850s the Geysers was developed into a spa with a resort hotel. In 1862, a rich businessman named Samuel Brannan (1819-89) opened another resort nearby, which he called Calistoga. There was a luxury hotel, with bathhouses for rich guests, and soon there was a railway service from San Francisco. One of the most famous spa visitors was the writer Robert Louis Stevenson. In 1881, Calistoga made headlines in national newspapers, when a man named Anson Tichenor claimed he had invented a way to extract gold from its hot springs. Unfortunately for Tichenor and Brannan, the invention was a fraud.

The Idaho State Capitol building in the city of Boise is heated by a geothermal well. The building was completed in 1920.

Do springs ever dry up?

If there is a good source of rainwater seeping down to the natural reservoir, this is unlikely. However, geological changes and rock movements can change underground formations. If too much hot water and steam are taken out through manmade boreholes, underground reserves can fall. In the region around Larderello, experts found in recent years that steam pressure had fallen. Investigations revealed that underground reserves of thermal water have dropped by nearly a third since the 1950s. This has led the energy company responsible for the area to drill twice as deep, to 4000 metres below ground, to find hotter sources.

Heating for homes

During the nineteenth century American engineers worked on ways of using geothermal water and steam. In 1892 a water company in Boise, the state capital of Idaho, offered to supply houses with hot water from two geothermal wells just outside the city. The company also built a geothermally heated natatorium (or swimming pool). Within a few years

Francesco Larderel

The French-born entrepreneur Francesco Larderel (1789-1858) set up a plant to extract a chemical called boric acid in a region of hot springs near the Tuscan city of Siena, in northern Italy. At first Larderel burned wood as fuel to boil water and volcanic mud from the springs, which contained a form of the mineral boron. Then, in 1827, he developed a way of using geothermal steam instead of burning wood. Before long, he was able to use the steam to drive well drills and pumps. This was the first time geothermal power was used for industrial purposes. Today there is a Geothermal Museum in Larderello, the town named after the entrepreneur, which commemorates his pioneering work.

There is still a geothermal plant at Larderello, in Italy.

the system was supplying 200 homes, as well as many businesses. A similar system still operates in Boise, extracting nearly 2.3 billion litres of geothermal water at a temperature of about 68°C.

First geo-electricity

The chemical works at Larderello continued after the founder's death, and in 1904 there was a fundamental change in the way the region used geothermal energy. The head of the company, Prince Piero Ginori Conti, used steam from the fumaroles to drive a dynamo (or simple generator) that produced enough electricity to illuminate five light bulbs. This may not seem very much, but it demonstrated that geothermal electricity was a possibility. It led to the development of a larger electrical plant a few years later, at a nearby site known as Devil's Valley.

Geothermal heating

We can use hot water from geothermal springs in heating systems. This is a direct use of geothermal power. The thermal water circulates through pipes, just as heated water does in a heating system fired by oil or gas. Or the thermal water can be used to heat cold water for the same purpose. This system is used when the thermal water contains such a high level of minerals that it would clog up water pipes.

Who uses geothermal power?

Geothermal heating systems can be used in homes and for many industrial purposes. Many countries use geothermal energy directly. The biggest users are shown in the chart below, which includes their percentage of world use. But these figures are slightly misleading. The United States and China are huge countries with large populations (China has more than 1330 million people). At the other end of the scale, Iceland has 0.3 million and Switzerland 7.6 million people. This means that Iceland produces the most geothermal energy per person – 68 times more than Switzerland, which comes second in the per person list. Hungary is third, Sweden fourth and the United States fifth.

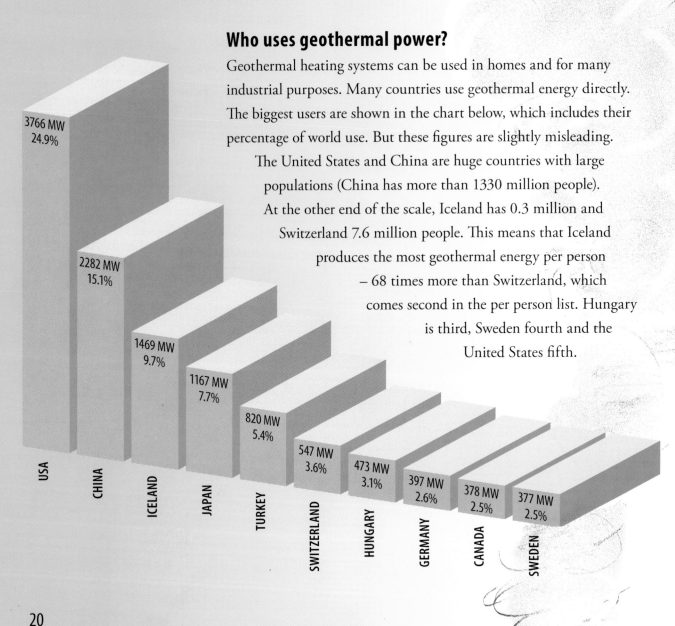

USA	3766 MW / 24.9%
CHINA	2282 MW / 15.1%
ICELAND	1469 MW / 9.7%
JAPAN	1167 MW / 7.7%
TURKEY	820 MW / 5.4%
SWITZERLAND	547 MW / 3.6%
HUNGARY	473 MW / 3.1%
GERMANY	397 MW / 2.6%
CANADA	378 MW / 2.5%
SWEDEN	377 MW / 2.5%

Land of fire and ice

The people who first settled on the island of Iceland, around 870, called their main settlement Reykjavik, which means 'smoky bay'. They saw what they thought was smoke coming out of the ground, but in fact this was steam from hot springs and fumaroles. Today, tourist operators call Iceland the land of fire and ice. The island lies just below the Arctic Circle and has many icy glaciers, but it is also an active volcanic region. According to ancient records, people used hot springs for washing and bathing. The first man-made wells for collecting hot water were sunk in 1756. By 1930, people were heating a school, a hospital and 60 homes in Reykjavik with thermal water.

Why does Iceland have so much geothermal power?

Iceland is special in terms of geothermal activity. It is a volcanic island, with more than 200 active volcanoes and 600 hot springs. As the Icelandic Tourist Board puts it: 'Situated on the Mid-Atlantic Ridge, Iceland is a hot spot of volcanic and geothermal activity: 30 post-glacial volcanoes have erupted in the past two centuries, and natural hot water supplies much of the population with cheap, pollution-free heating.' So there is plenty of thermal water and it flows at a fast rate, making it easy to send along pipes. The Icelandic hot spring called Deildartunguhver has Europe's highest flow rate (at 180 litres per second) and provides water at 97°C, which is piped up to 64 kilometres to heat towns and villages.

Large pipes lead from a geothermal plant in New Zealand, which uses almost as much direct thermal heating as Sweden (see the chart opposite).

Hotter and cooler areas

Geothermal areas in Iceland are divided into high-temperature and low-temperature fields. The dividing point is 150°C. High-temperature fields measure at least 150°C at a depth of 1000 metres and they are in the active volcanic zone. This runs along the tectonic plate boundaries of the Mid-Atlantic Ridge (see page 11). Hot magma chambers supply the fumaroles, mud pots and hot springs in these areas and the water temperature rises to 350°C at about 2000 metres below the ground. The Nesjavellir high-temperature field produces water at 250-300°C. Experts have identified 28 high-temperature fields in Iceland, as well as 250 low-temperature fields.

Building up a system

During the 1930s, engineers drilled 32 boreholes in a geothermal area of Iceland about 17 kilometres east of Reykjavik. By 1940 engineers were laying a pipeline from the boreholes to the capital and building a large storage tank for the thermal water, which had a temperature of 86°C. By the 1950s half of Reykjavik's

Steam rises from a pipeline near the Nesjavellir geothermal plant in Iceland.

What is it used for?

Here is a breakdown of how people in Iceland use geothermal energy.

Space heating (homes)	57.4%
Electricity generation	15.9%
Fish farming	10.4%
Snow melting	5.4%
Industry	4.7%
Swimming pools	3.7%
Greenhouses	2.5%.

citizens had access to hot geothermal water. More boreholes were sunk in other areas, and by 1972 nearly everyone had geothermal heating.

How the Reykjavik system works

Hot water is pumped out of boreholes from about 200 metres underground by electric motors. The water is pumped through 90-cm wide pipes and then flows downhill by gravity to the city's six large storage tanks. Then it is pumped through narrower pipes to districts, streets and individual homes. Customers can control how much hot water they use which is measured by their water meter. The water passes through radiators and into hot-water tanks and taps, so that people can wash and bathe in it too. Most of the used water then flows into rainwater drains. Some heating water is returned to a pumping station, where it is mixed with very hot water to bring it down to the working temperature of 80°C.

Melting snow and ice

Once the hot water has travelled through a heating system, it has a temperature of 25-40°C. In winter some of it is pumped into tanks and pipes which are used to clear roads and pavements of snow and ice. In Reykjavik, the average temperature is -1°C in January and 11°C in July, so heating is needed all year round.

Cutting pollution

Using geothermal power can help to reduce air pollution. Before the mid-twentieth century, the main source of heat and power in Reykjavik was coal. Burning coal gave off so much waste gas that a cloud of black smoke often hung over the city. This air pollution also added to the greenhouse effect that is causing global warming (see page 35). In 1960 about 250,000 tonnes of the greenhouse gas called carbon dioxide were sent into the atmosphere just by heating Reykjavik. By 1975 this amount was reduced to about 20,000 tonnes a year, and today it is virtually nil.

The city of Reykjavik, on the south-west coast of Iceland, lies next to snow-covered mountains.

The Blue Lagoon

One of the world's most popular geothermal spots is a lake of waste water from an Icelandic power plant. The Svartsengi plant in south-west Iceland lies above a large geothermal reservoir. Water seeps into the reservoir from the nearby sea, so it is salty. The plant has wells up to 2000 metres deep, which produce steam and 475 litres per second of 90°C hot water. This is used to drive turbines and produce electricity, before passing through an exchanger to heat water which heats nearby communities. Finally, the water passes into a large pool known as the Blue Lagoon, which looks blue because of microscopic algae in the water. By then the water is about 40°C, a very pleasant temperature for bathing in cold Iceland. The warm water is rich in silica, sulphur and other minerals, and the lagoon has become a health resort as well as a bathing pool. People claim that the water is especially soothing for skin problems.

Good for you?

The Blue Lagoon operators claim that their mineral-rich waters are very healthy. They encourage visitors to apply the volcanic mud at the bottom of the pool. Their website states: 'Guests enjoy bathing and relaxing in Blue Lagoon geothermal seawater, known for its positive effects on the skin. A visit to the spa promotes harmony between body, mind and spirit, and enables one to soak away the stresses of modern life. The spa's guests rekindle their relationship with nature, soak up the scenic beauty and enjoy breathing the clean, fresh air.'

Bathers enjoy the warm geothermal waters of the Blue Lagoon, in Iceland.

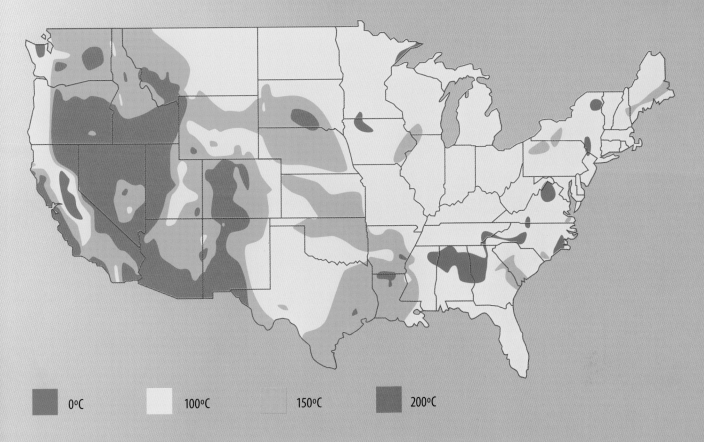

0ºC	100ºC	150ºC	200ºC

World's biggest producer

The United States produces nearly a quarter of the world's geothermal power for direct use. As the map shows, most geothermal areas are in the west of the country. According to the US Department of Energy, a recent survey of western states found more than 9000 thermal wells and springs, more than 900 low- to moderate-temperature geothermal areas, and hundreds of direct-use sites. The survey also identified 271 western towns and communities within eight kilometres of a usable geothermal site, with a total population of 7.4 million. Experts calculate that if geothermal resources were used to heat buildings in the 271 communities, 18 million barrels of oil a year would be saved.

A map produced by the US Department of Energy which shows estimated underground temperatures in the United States at a depth of six kilometres.

Farmers and gardeners

Geothermal energy is particularly useful for farmers and gardeners. Hot-water pipes provide heat for greenhouses and even under-soil heating for fields. This allows growers to cultivate vegetables, flowers and tree seedlings out of season or in a cold climate. Fish farms use the warm water to breed tropical fish in cooler waters. In Idaho, one geothermal fish farm even has some warm outdoor ponds for breeding alligators. The farm has no pumps, pipes or heat exchangers, so the operating cost of the geothermal system is zero.

Pumping heat

The top few metres of the Earth's surface stay at a relatively constant temperature all year round. The ground is generally warmer than the air above it during winter, remaining at about 10-16°C. A geothermal heat pump takes advantage of this source of warmth by transferring it into a building. During the warm summer months, the system can work the other way, taking heat from the building and transferring it to the ground, which acts as a heat sink. So the pump heats a building in winter and cools it in summer. It can also be used to run a hot-water system.

Low temperature underfloor heating

Heat pump

Hot-water tank

Underground loop

This diagram of a geothermal heat-pump system shows cold water (blue) being pumped underground and returning warm (red). The hot water can be used throughout the house.

What's in a name?

Geothermal heat pump (GHP) systems are also known as ground-source or ground-coupled heat pumps, water-source heat pumps (as opposed to air-source) or geo-exchange systems. Many different companies sell and install the technology for homeowners, and some have made up their own trade names.

Looping down

To pick up geothermal heat, a length of plastic pipe – called a loop – is buried in the ground near the building. The loop can be placed either vertically or horizontally. An antifreeze solution is pumped through the pipe by an electric pump. The antifreeze is heated by the ground as it passes through it on its way to the heat pump inside the building. This pump, which also runs on electricity, has a heat exchanger that takes heat from the solution to warm air that it pumps throughout the building. Alternatively, it can be used to pump warm water around a series of radiators. The cool antifreeze solution then flows back through the underground loop to pick up more heat.

Environmental benefits

According to the Geothermal Heat Pump Consortium, GHPs are having a huge effect on the environment. In the United States alone, there are more than a million GHP installations. The consortium says that using them saves 21.5 million barrels of crude oil and cuts CO_2 emissions by 5.8 million tonnes. In terms of reducing greenhouse gases, this is equivalent to taking nearly 1.3 million cars off the road or planting more than 385 million trees.

Are heat pumps expensive?

The initial cost of installing a geothermal heat pump system can be two or three times more than a gas heating system. But the geo-system cuts heating (and cooling) costs by 35-70 per cent. This means that the system usually pays for itself in three to five years. The average lifespan of a pump is around 22 years, and loops should last at least 50 years.

As well as saving money, geo-pumps have other advantages. The US Environmental Protection Agency calls them 'the most energy-efficient, environmentally clean, cost-effective space conditioning systems available'. Geo-pumps started to become popular in the 1980s and have become more appealing in the twenty-first century, as the price of oil and gas has continued to rise. Apart from a small amount of electricity, the heat pump uses free geothermal energy.

Generating electricity

Geothermal steam and hot water can drive generators and produce electricity as well as being used for heating systems. This technology was first introduced in Italy in 1904 (see page 19) and was developed further around the world during the twentieth century. Today, geo-electricity makes up less than one per cent of total global production, but that still means that it supplies electricity to around 60 million people.

Turbines and generators

Electricity generation started in the nineteenth century. In 1831 the British scientist Michael Faraday (1791-1867) discovered that he could create electricity by moving a magnet through a coil of copper wire. This process, called electromagnetic induction, led to the invention of the electric generator, which works by changing mechanical energy into electrical energy. In geothermal power plants, steam provides the mechanical energy by turning the rotor blades of a turbine. The blades are connected to a shaft, which is also attached to a generator. Inside the generator, the shaft makes magnets spin inside wire coils to produce electricity.

Top ten

Here is a list of the world's top geo-electricity producers. Compare this list with the one on page 20. Only three countries appear in both lists: the USA, Japan and Iceland.

USA	Philippines	Mexico	Indonesia	Italy	Japan	New Zealand	Iceland	Costa Rica	El Salvador
2544 MW 28.1%	1931 MW 21.3%	953 MW 10.5%	797 MW 8.8%	790 MW 8.7%	535 MW 5.9%	435 MW 4.8%	322 MW 3.6%	163 MW 1.8%	151 MW 1.7%

FLASH-STEAM POWER PLANT

How the power plant works

Steam power plants use geothermal steam and hot water. In dry steam plants, the steam comes directly from the geothermal source and is used to turn the turbine. Increased pressure raises a liquid's boiling point, which means that water can be much hotter than 100°C underground and still be a liquid. In a flash-steam power plant, very hot, high-pressure water is flashed (or depressurized) to produce steam. The steam then turns a turbine, which drives a generator that produces electricity.

In a flash-steam plant, as in other geothermal plants, heat is used both to produce electricity and for direct heating. Used water is returned underground so the well does not dry up.

Does geothermal power pollute the air?

Geothermal power plants emit mainly water vapour (as steam), which is a greenhouse gas but is not believed very damaging to the atmosphere. Some people worry about hydrogen sulphide, (which smells like rotten eggs) found in all geothermal areas. Minute amounts of carbon dioxide, nitric oxide, and sulphur are emitted. There may also be other minerals released along with steam. The magazine *Renewable Energy World* says: 'When it comes to the environmental benefits of using geothermal for power production, the majority of emissions from a geothermal source are water vapour. A coal plant with scrubbers and other emissions control technologies can emit 24 times more carbon dioxide, 10,837 times more sulphur dioxide, and 3865 times more nitrous oxides per megawatt hour than a geothermal steam plant, according to the GEA [Geothermal Energy Association].'

A two-part system

Binary plants use a different system and are useful where there is a supply of hot geothermal water rather than steam. The hot water passes through a heat exchanger containing a fluid with a lower boiling point, such as isobutane. The fluid vaporizes, and the vapour turns the turbine, which drives the generator. The remaining secondary fluid is recycled through the heat exchanger. The geothermal water is returned to the reservoir. Binary plants are closed (or self-contained), so they do not emit gases.

World's largest power plants

The biggest series of geothermal power plants in the world is in the Mayacamas Mountains, a 78 sq km region of California, 115 kilometres north of San Francisco. The area is called the Geysers, and fumaroles were found there in the nineteenth century (see page 17). In 1921 America's first geothermal plant went into operation, producing electricity to light the spa resort there. In 1960 a large commercial plant opened at the Geysers, producing 11 MW of power. Today there are 21 separate power plants using steam from more than 350 geothermal wells. Together they generate more than 725 MW of electricity – enough to power 725,000 homes across five Californian counties.

What is a watt?

A watt (W) is a unit of power, which measures the rate of producing or using energy. The term was named after the Scottish engineer James Watt (1736-1819), who developed an improved steam engine. Watt himself measured his engine's performance in horsepower (hp). One horsepower equals 746 watts. Today, watts are generally used to measure electric power.

1 kilowatt (kW) = 1 thousand watts
1 megawatt (MW) = 1 million watts
1 gigawatt (GW) = 1 thousand million watts.

One of the electric power plants at the Geysers, California.

Mud pots bubble near one of the Geysers power plants.

From the depths

Geological studies suggest that the heat source for the Geysers is a 14-km wide magma chamber that lies about seven kilometres beneath the surface. This volcanic region is connected to the famous San Andreas Fault, which is responsible for many Californian earthquakes.

Recycling power

The Geysers area was developed very rapidly in the 1980s, and by 1990 the total capacity had risen to 2000 MW. As in other dry steam plants, some of the steam condenses to water after passing through the turbine and is put back below ground through a separate injection well. Nevertheless, around two thirds of the steam goes up into the atmosphere, and the underground steam pressure has been steadily dropping. Projects are under way to introduce more water to the underground reservoir.

Do geo-plants produce electricity all the time?

Hot springs and thermal wells produce heat continuously, so in theory geothermal power plants can generate electricity all the time. In practice, there is a small amount of downtime for servicing. As the environmental group Greenpeace puts it: 'Geothermal power generation causes virtually no pollution or greenhouse gas emissions. It's also quiet, and extremely reliable. Geothermal power plants produce electricity about 90 per cent of the time, compared to 65-75 per cent for fossil fuel power plants. Unfortunately, even in many countries with abundant geothermal reserves, this proven renewable energy source is being massively underutilized.'

GEOTHERMAL POWER

Hot rocks

Scientists have been working for many years on technology known as hot dry rock (or HDR). When geologists find a suitable area, engineers drill down to where the underground rocks are hot but there is little or no water. Water is pumped down into this borehole (called an injection well), and this opens small cracks in the bed of hot rocks, making a thermal reservoir. Then engineers drill a second borehole (called a production well), so that the heated water comes back up to the surface, as it does in a natural geyser. The HDR pressurized hot water can be used to heat another liquid in a heat exchanger, before it is returned underground through the injection well to regain its geothermal heat. Steam from the heat exchanger can drive a turbine and generate electricity in the same way as in other power plants.

This illustration shows how an HDR system works. Could this be the future for geothermal power?

American research

American scientists began a large research programme in 1971, at Fenton Hill in the Jemez Mountains of New Mexico. Fenton Hill is the site of a dormant volcano that probably last erupted 60,000 years ago. After surveying the area, engineers drilled a borehole nearly 3000 metres deep into a bedrock of granite, where the temperature was 197°C. In 1980 German and Japanese scientists joined the project, and drilled a deeper borehole down to 4390 metres, where the temperature was 327°C. They pumped water into the reservoir over several days, and drilled a production well which proved that the technology worked. However, the project had finished by 1996, when the Fenton Hill site was closed. Nevertheless, the scientists had learned a great deal about HDR.

Power plant

Cooling unit

Reservoir

Heat exchanger

Production wells

Injection well

Sediments

Crystalline rocks

This is the drill derrick for the Swiss Deep Heat Mining project in Basel. Work was stopped after earth tremors were felt in Basel. A decision on further work depends on the outcome of investigations.

Swiss tremors

The Deep Heat Mining project aims to set up a geothermal power plant in Basel, Switzerland in the near future. The plant should be able to generate 20,000 megawatt-hours of electricity per year, and 80,000 megawatt-hours of heating. In December 2006 engineers started pumping water into a five-kilometre deep borehole, but within days a small earthquake was reported in the nearby city of Basel. The quake measured 3.4 on the Richter scale and caused minor damage to some buildings. Water pumping was stopped at once, but more tremors were felt later. People were particularly worried because Basel was flattened by a huge earthquake in 1356.

Is geothermal technology dangerous?

It is not yet far enough advanced to answer this question. There is always an element of danger when engineers drill or mine underground, because rocks move and fractures can cause tremors. Minor earthquakes have been caused by filling reservoirs with water, so it is possible that pumping water deep underground could also have this effect. The Basel incident confirmed this, and small tremors have been noted during other HDR programmes, including the US Fenton Hill project. Scientists have learned a great deal from these incidents, which should help to make the technology safer in future.

Australian granite

Scientists at the University of New South Wales began working on HDR in 1993. Since then interest has grown throughout Australia, and 32 companies had applied for licences to drill in geothermal areas by 2008. In the state of South Australia alone, 22 companies have applied for more than 200 licences covering a geothermal area of more than 80,000 square kilometres. Two of the best areas are thought to be the Cooper Basin area of South Australia and the Hunter Valley of New South Wales. In 2008, one company reached its target borehole depth of 4222 metres and hopes to produce HDR geothermal electricity in the near future.

Huge research costs

One of the problems with geo-electricity is that HDR and similar technologies cost a great deal to research. Ideally, governments and international agencies would undertake research and development, because individual companies do not want to spend the money without guaranteed rewards. The environmental group Envocare is convinced that more money needs to be spent: 'Internationally the quantity of geothermal energy is virtually infinite and the environmental benefits are beyond reproach. Set against this are the disadvantages that considerably more research and development are needed to take advantage of the buried wealth, and even when a commercially viable site is identified,

Unlimited heat resource

The Australian energy company Geodynamics believes that Australia has large volumes of hot granite rocks between three and five kilometres beneath the surface. The company believes that one cubic kilometre of hot granite at 250°C has the same amount of stored energy as 40 million barrels of oil. It states: 'This represents a vast resource of clean energy that can potentially be tapped by hot fractured rock geothermal technology.' Hot fractured rock (HFR) is another term for HDR, and is so called because the injected water fractures, or further splits, tiny cracks in underground rocks.

Renewable resource

Geothermal energy is called a renewable resource, because we do not reduce stocks of it by using it. This means there is never any danger of the resource running out.

the initial investment cost can be a serious deterrent. Maybe if some of the multinationals that have the resources to invest in oil exploration could channel them into geothermal exploration, research and development, we might see geothermal energy being tapped on a significant scale. But then we're prejudiced, aren't we?'

A geothermal expert takes a close look at a hot spring in Yellowstone National Park, USA.

Geothermal power and global warming

The Earth's atmosphere prevents some of the Sun's rays from reaching Earth. Its gases also stop some heat escaping from Earth, just as glass traps warmth inside a greenhouse. We add to this natural greenhouse effect by emitting so many waste gases from power plants, factories and cars. Many of these greenhouse gases — especially carbon dioxide — are produced when we burn coal, oil or gas to release energy. Experts have discovered that in this way humans are making natural climate change more extreme. Much of our energy use adds to global warming, so that land, sea and air temperatures are gradually increasing. Using energy from renewable sources — such as geothermal energy — can help to reduce the increase in global warming.

Geothermal energy around the world

Geothermal energy – the Earth's heat – comes through the planet's crust to its surface all over the world. This means that geothermal power can be tapped into on all the world's continents. However, there is much more accessible power in volcanic regions with a lot of tectonic activity, such as the Pacific rim known as the Ring of Fire (see page 10).

In the early twenty-first century North America produces more electricity from geothermal sources than any other continent. Next comes Asia, where the largest electricity producer is the Philippines and the biggest direct user is China.

Island countries

Geo-power is growing fast in the island countries of southeast Asia. Research began in the Philippines in the 1970s, and the first commercial power plant began operating in 1977. Today, geo-power generates a quarter of the country's electricity, and there are plants on Luzon, Leyte and other main islands, with cables on the Pacific seabed to connect them. Geothermal heat is also used directly in the Philippines to process fish, to dry fruit and to desalinate water (remove salt from seawater).

Further south, Indonesia is also using more geothermal energy. In 2004, a total of 18 power plants produced 807 MW of geothermal power, which made up 60 per cent of its power from renewable sources and two per cent of its total power production. By 2025 Indonesia is aiming to have at least 13 more plants and to increase the geothermal total to 9500 MW (44 per cent of its renewable energy and four per cent of the total).

Geo in Japan

The islands of Japan lie where four of the planet's tectonic plates meet – the Eurasian and North American plates to the north, and the Philippine and Pacific plates to the south. So it is not surprising that Japan has many volcanoes and experiences about 1000 earthquakes every year. Japan also has a long tradition of using its thermal resources. One city famous for its spas and bathhouses is Beppu, which has eight major hot springs. They have become a tourist attraction for Japanese and international visitors.

Japan began using geothermal electricity in 1966, and by 1982 it had seven geothermal power plants. One of the problems in Japan is that the hot springs are in areas that have become national parks, and this makes it difficult for industry to develop further. Environmentalists understandably oppose development in these areas, but this means that renewable resources cannot be fully exploited.

Bathing at a thermal pool in Beppu, Japan.

Tapping potential energy

Geological researchers in southeast Asia are certain there is much more geothermal energy to be tapped. A study in Indonesia showed that production is three per cent of what it could be. In Iceland too (see pages 20-24), there is still more potential. The Icelandic National Energy Authority says, 'Only 20 to 25 per cent of the technically and environmentally feasible hydropower, and only 20 per cent of the conventional geothermal potential available for electricity production in Iceland have been harnessed.' In the US, the Geological Survey estimates that less than two per cent of potential geothermal energy is currently used.

GEOTHERMAL POWER

Fifty years of progress

At the south-western end of the Pacific rim there is a great deal of volcanic activity in New Zealand. The first geothermal plant was opened in 1957 in the Taupo volcanic zone of the North Island, where magma rises close to the surface. This raises the temperature to at least 350°C at depths of less than five kilometres. There are 29 geothermal areas here, and 100 more in the rest of the country. Each field covers about 12 square kilometres, and many spout boiling water as well as steam. There are plans to build a geothermal plant at the Kawerau field, 25 kilometres from the Bay of Plenty on the Pacific Ocean. The Kawerau plant will be the largest geothermal power project in New Zealand since 1989 and will increase the country's geothermal capacity by a quarter.

Overcoming problems

Like all power plants, geothermal units can break down. This happened to an African geothermal generator, the 8.5-MW Aluto-Langano plant in Ethiopia. It started generating in 1999, but technical problems forced it to stop operations in 2002. While it is being repaired and checked, engineers are taking the opportunity to increase its production capacity to 30 MW.

Demonstrators protest against a geothermal project in Hawaii (see opposite).

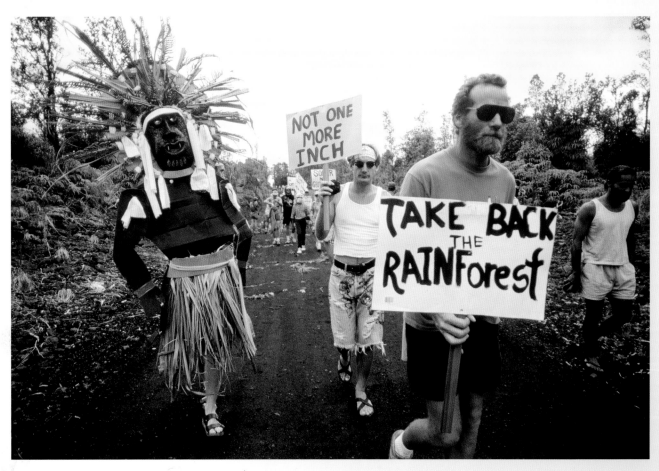

38

No to geo!

Building geothermal plants in national parks and places of scenic interest can divide public opinion. One project in Hawaii caused huge protests and demonstrations. Some protesters carried banners that read 'Just say no to geo!' The project was a power plant planned for the 104-square kilometre Wao Kele O Puna (green forest of Puna), the largest rainforest in the United States. Community groups gathered to protect the forest, which has been traditionally used for hunting, gathering and religious purposes. It is also home to 200 native Hawaiian animal and plant species, including many considered endangered. In 2006 the Office of Hawaiian Affairs announced that it had bought the forest and that it would not be developed.

Geo-power in East Africa

The Great Rift Valley, in East Africa, is another region where moving plates have caused geothermal activity. The rift stretches for about 7000 kilometres, where there are valleys filled with lakes bounded by volcanic mountains. As yet there is little geothermal power production in Africa, but Kenya and Ethiopia – both on the eastern branch of the rift – have opened plants.

The Olkaria power plant is made up of three units in Hell's Gate National Park near Kenya's Lake Naivasha. The first was opened in 1981, and today the plants have 110 thermal wells drilled down to 1300 metres. Altogether the Olkaria geothermal field covers 70 square kilometres. The United Nations believes that geothermal energy in developing countries such as Kenya will reduce the need for fossil fuels or hydropower which can be affected by the dry season. Geothermal provides 11 per cent of Kenya's power, and experts say there is the potential to generate much more.

Geothermal power production in the East African country of Kenya. Demand for electricity is growing at eight per cent a year in Kenya. Energy experts predict that geothermal power will help to supply the increased demand.

What does the future hold?

Experts agree that all renewable sources of energy
– including geothermal – will become more important
and that we will use them more in future. Forecasts
predict that demand for electricity will double over
the next 25 years, stretching current resources.

Politicians want to convince voters that there will not be
shortages of electricity or fuels, especially for transport. At the same time,
environmentalists will continue to be concerned that energy policies do
not increase pollution or contribute further to global warming. These
concerns place geothermal power in a strong position compared with
fossil fuels.

Improving the technology

The technology of Enhanced Geothermal Systems (or EGS) includes
Hot Dry Rock (or HDR, see page 32). The systems are called enhanced
(meaning increased) because they add water from the surface to the
natural thermal water that is already underground. There are some
concerns about this, especially the possibility of triggering earthquakes
(see page 33), but the technology will improve in the coming decades.
There are EGS research projects in many parts of the world.

Time for action

A group of experts at Massachusetts Institute of Technology (MIT)
undertook a study of EGS in 2005. Their conclusion was that immediate
action is needed: 'Because prototype commercial-scale EGS will take a
few years to develop and field-test, the time for action is now. Supporting
the EGS program now will move us along the learning curve to a point
where the design and engineering of well-connected EGS reservoir
systems is technically reliable and reproducible... The payoff for EGS

Members of the Australian Greens party dressed as lifesavers for a demonstration in Sydney. They want to save the planet by doing everything they can to prevent further global warming.

is large, especially in the light of how much will have to be spent for deployment of conventional gas, nuclear, or coal-fired systems to meet replacement of retiring plants and capacity increases, as there are no other options with sufficient scale on the horizon... Like all new energy-supply technologies, for EGS to enter and compete in evolving US electricity markets, positive policies at the state and federal levels will be required. These policies must be similar to those that oil and gas and other mineral-extraction operations have received in the past.'

What about cost?

People are concerned about the cost of energy, especially electricity. One of the problems with large geothermal projects is that the initial costs are high. This means that electricity from geothermal sources costs more to produce than electricity from sources such as fossil fuels. In some countries, geothermal and other renewable sources are helped to compete with fossil fuels by what is called a feed-in tariff. This is the price per unit of electricity that a national or regional energy supplier has to pay for renewable electricity (including geothermal) from private generators. The government sets the tariff (or price), and in Germany, for example, this is covered by a Renewable Energy Law. This helps new energy-generating companies compete with traditional suppliers. Once the initial costs have been paid off, geothermal energy should be very cheap.

These lettuces are growing in a geothermally-heated greenhouse at Chena Hot Springs in Alaska, USA. The greenhouse is near a low-temperature geothermal power plant (see panel opposite).

Using waste gas

An American scientist has proposed pumping waste carbon dioxide gas into thermal reservoirs. Under high pressure, the CO_2 would act as a fluid and replace water in an HDR system (see page 32). The CO_2 would stay in a closed system, so it would not escape into the air. The waste gas could come from sources such as coal- or gas-fired power stations, and this use would help combat the greenhouse effect and global warming. The scientist has been granted a patent on his version of this process.

Community projects

There could be many more small-scale community projects. One project opened in 2007 in Unterhaching, a town south of Munich in Germany, where thermal hot water is piped from 3300 metres underground to heat local houses. In Germany's capital, Berlin, the national parliament building has its own geothermal system. In summer waste heat is pumped down to a natural water reservoir in sandstone 320 metres below ground. In winter, hot water (70°C) is brought up to heat the large building.

Make it international

Sharing information will help the development of geothermal technology, especially if industrialized countries share their knowledge with developing nations. The results of research and development can be shared through the International Geothermal Association (IGA), which was founded in 1988 and has headquarters in Reykjavik, Iceland. The IGA has more than 2000 members in 65 countries and has strong connections with the United Nations organization. The association organizes World Geothermal Congresses, and the next one is scheduled for 2010 in Bali, Indonesia.

Fuel cells

Another development could be in hydrogen-powered fuel cells. These generate electricity to run vehicles such as cars. All that is needed are hydrogen and oxygen, with water as a harmless by-product. The problem is that it takes a lot of energy to split hydrogen from water or hydrocarbons. Scientists are finding ways of using geothermal power to provide this energy, which would make producing hydrogen easy and relatively cheap. This could be a major step in reducing fossil fuels burned for transport.

Planning a mix of energy sources

After reading all the facts about geothermal power, including its potential, do you think this should be the sole solution to our energy needs in the future? Many experts believe it would be better to view it as one element in an energy mix of renewable resources (biomass, geothermal, solar, water and wind) and non-renewable sources (fossil fuels and nuclear energy). That way we should avoid the possibility of an energy gap, but at the same time make sure that the energy we use and the electricity we generate are less harmful to the environment.

Glossary

asthenosphere   A zone in the upper part of the Earth's mantle.

carbon dioxide (CO_2)   A greenhouse gas given off when fossil fuels are burned.

climate change   A change in general weather conditions over a long period of time, including higher temperatures, more or less rain, droughts, etc.

condense   To change from a gas into a liquid (as steam into water).

conductor   A substance that allows something such as heat to pass along or through it.

constructive margin   A divergent margin.

continental plate   A tectonic plate beneath the land of a continent.

convergent margin   A boundary between tectonic plates where one plate dips beneath another.

derrick   A framework that supports drilling equipment.

destructive margin   A convergent margin.

divergent margin   A boundary between tectonic plates where new crust is formed.

dormant   Inactive.

dynamo   A machine that turns mechanical energy into electrical energy.

electromagnetic induction   The process of creating electricity by using magnetic forces.

emission   Producing and giving off something (such as a waste gas); also, the waste gas produced and given off.

fumarole   A hole in the ground that releases geothermal steam and volcanic gases.

geologist   A scientist who studies the structure of the Earth.

geyser   A hot spring where boiling water and steam regularly shoot up high in the air.

global warming   Heating up of the Earth's surface, especially caused by pollution from burning fossil fuels.

greenhouse effect   Warming of the Earth's surface caused especially by pollution from burning fossil fuels.

greenhouse gas   A gas, such as carbon dioxide, that traps heat from the sun near the Earth and helps to create the greenhouse effect.

hydrogen sulphide   A flammable gas with a characteristic smell of rotten eggs.

isobutane   A gaseous substance that can be used as a fuel.

magma   Molten rock formed in the Earth's mantle.

mantle   The thick layer of molten rock beneath the Earth's crust.

mechanical energy   The energy that something has because of its position (potential energy) and its movement (kinetic energy). Also, the energy transmitted by a machine.

mineral   A solid chemical substance that occurs naturally in the Earth.

mud pot   A place where geothermal steam bubbles through a surface layer of mud.

nickel   A hard silvery-white metal.

nitric oxide   A colourless poisonous gas.

ocean crust   Earth's crust beneath an ocean.

oceanic plate   A tectonic plate beneath the waters of an ocean.

radioactive decay   The process by which substances with unstable atoms (such as uranium) give off energy.

renewable resources   Sources of energy that do not run out by being used, such as biomass, geothermal, solar, water and wind power.

Richter scale   A scale from 1 to 10 used to measure the strength of earthquakes.

scrubber   A device that filters and cleans harmful fumes.

silica   A hard mineral (silicon dioxide).

subduction zone   The region of a convergent margin where one tectonic plate dips beneath another.

tectonic plate   One of the large pieces of the Earth's crust.

United Nations   An international organization that promotes peace and security.

uranium   A radioactive metal that is used to produce nuclear power.

vaporize   To change into a vapour (or gas).

Websites

The International Geothermal Association (IGA) website has facts, data and opinions
http://iga.igg.cnr.it

The US Department of Energy's Geothermal Technologies Program
www1.eere.energy.gov/geothermal

The environmental benefits of geothermal energy from the Geothermal Energy Association
www.geo-energy.org/aboutGE/environment.asp#airemissions

A case study on geothermal energy in Erding, Germany
www.managenergy.net/products/R444.htm

A fascinating video by Schreiner Productions on geothermal energy in Iceland
www.youtube.com/watch?v=XRAQrDduaU0

Index